PRESENTED TO

_____

FROM

_____

By Helen Steiner Rice

Heart Gifts From Helen Steiner Rice
Lovingly, Helen Steiner Rice
Someone Cares
The Story of the Christmas Guest
Loving Promises
A Gift of Love
Everyone Needs Someone
Somebody Loves You
Love
In the Vineyard of the Lord
Mothers Are a Gift of Love
Gifts From the Heart
Loving Thoughts
Remembering With Love
A Time to Love
Always a Springtime
Celebrations of the Heart

CELEBRATIONS
OF THE HEART

HELEN STEINER RICE

Fleming H. Revell Company
Old Tappan, New Jersey

Library of Congress Cataloging-in-Publication Data

Rice, Helen Steiner.
    Celebrations of the heart.

    I. Title.
PS3568.I28C4   1987   811'.54   87-16272
ISBN 0-8007-1553-5

Copyright © 1987 by The Helen Steiner Rice Foundation
Published by the Fleming H. Revell Company
Old Tappan, New Jersey 07675
Printed in the United States of America

Contents

A Word From the Author

We all need words to live by,
To inspire us and guide us,
Words to give us courage
When the trials of life betide us.
And the words that never fail us
Are the words of God above,
Words of comfort and of courage
Filled with wisdom and with love.
They are ageless and enduring,
They have lived through generations,
There's no question left unanswered
In our Father's revelations.
And in this ever-changing world
God's words remain unchanged,
For though through countless ages
They've been often rearranged,
The truth shines through all changes
Just as bright today as when
Our Father made the universe
And breathed His Life in men.
And the words of inspiration
That I write for you today
Are just the old enduring truths
Said in a rhythmic way.
And if my "borrowed words of truth"
In some way touch your heart,
Then I am deeply thankful
To have had a little part
In sharing these God-given lines,
And I hope you'll share them, too,
With family, friends, and loved ones
And all those dear to you.

HELEN STEINER RICE

Dedication

Dedicated to Responsive Hearts
wherever they may be,
For the love and inspiration
they keep giving generously.
For the things that I have written
do not belong to me,
They reflect the many people
who have quite unconsciously
Inspired my life and writings
in a myriad of ways
And encouraged all my efforts
with their warm and generous praise.
So each book is a tribute
for little daily graces
That have come to me across the world
from little-dreamed-of places.

Whatever the celebration, whatever the day, whatever the event, whatever the occasion, Helen Steiner Rice possessed the ability to express the appropriate feeling for that particular moment in time.

A happening became happier, a sentiment more sentimental, a memory more memorable because of her deep sensitivity to put into understandable language the emotion being experienced. Her positive attitude, her concern for others, and her love of God are identifiable threads woven into her life, her works . . . and even her death.

Prior to her passing, she established the HELEN STEINER RICE FOUNDATION, a nonprofit corporation whose purpose is to award grants to worthy charitable programs that aid the elderly, the needy, and the poor. In her lifetime, these were the individuals about whom Mrs. Rice was greatly concerned.

Royalties from the sale of this book will add to the financial capabilities of the HELEN STEINER RICE FOUNDATION, thus making possible additional grants. In the four years of its existence, the foundation has presented seventy-four grants, ranging from three thousand to fifteen thousand dollars each, to various, qualified, worthwhile, and charitable programs. Because of her foresight, her caring, and her deep convictions, Helen Steiner Rice continues to touch a countless number of lives. Thank you for your assistance in helping to keep Helen's dream alive.

Virginia J. Ruehlmann, Administrator
THE HELEN STEINER RICE FOUNDATION

CELEBRATIONS
OF THE HEART

SPRING

The Waking Earth

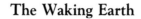

The waking earth in springtime
Reminds us it is true
That nothing really ever dies
That is not born anew.
So trust God's all-wise wisdom
And doubt the Father never,
For in His Heavenly Kingdom
There is nothing lost forever.

Beyond the Clouds

Most of the battles
of life are won
by looking
beyond the clouds
to the sun,
And having
the patience
to wait for the day
when the sun comes out
and the clouds
float away!

All nature heeds
the call of spring
As God awakens
everything.

Ireland Is the Land of Love, Legends, and Laughter

There are many, many legends
about Saint Patrick's Day,
About the Shamrock
and the Blarney
and the Leprechauns at play,
And that most delightful story
that God blessed
the Emerald Isle
With the beauty of His goodness
and the sunshine of His smile,
And how a dear, beloved Saint
taught the Irish about God
Just by showing them a Shamrock
that was grown on Erin's sod.
He told them of the Trinity,
the living Three in One,
The Holy Ghost, . . . the Father,
and His Beloved Son.
And all these lovely legends
of the well-loved Irish race
Have given every Irishman
A very special place
Not only just in history
but in everybody's heart,
For of this old earth's laughter,
the dearest, finest part
Is made of "smiling Irish eyes"
and mirth-filled Irish jokes
And what a dull world
this would be
without God's Irish folks.

Spring Song

"The earth is the Lord's
and the fulness thereof"
It speaks of His greatness
and it sings of His love,
And the wonder and glory
of the first Easter morn,
Like the first Christmas night
when the Saviour was born,
Are blended together
in symphonic splendor
And God with a voice
that is gentle and tender
Speaks to all hearts
attuned to His voice,
Bidding His listeners
to gladly rejoice.
For He who was born
to be crucified
Arose from the grave
to be glorified.
And the birds in the trees
and the flowers of spring
All join in proclaiming
this heavenly King.

A Spring Awakening

Spring is God's way
of speaking to men
And saying, "Through Me
you will live again."
For death is a season
that man must pass through
And, just like the flowers,
God awakens him, too.

Spring Awakens
What Autumn Puts to Sleep

A garden of asters of varying hues,
Crimson pinks and violet blues,
Blossoming in the hazy fall
Wrapped in autumn's lazy pall.
But early frost stole in one night
And like a chilling, killing blight
It touched each pretty aster's head
And now the garden's still and dead.
And all the lovely flowers that bloomed
Will soon be buried and entombed
In winter's icy shroud of snow
But, oh, how wonderful to know
That after winter comes the spring
To breathe new life in everything.
And all the flowers that fell in death
Will be awakened by spring's breath—
For in God's plan both men and flowers
Can only reach "bright, shining hours"
By dying first to rise in glory
And prove again the Easter story.

God Be With You
at Easter
and Always

The promise of Easter
is witnessed and heard
In each budding flower
and each singing bird,
For Easter and spring
are God's loving way
Of showing that He
is still with us today.

19

Eternal Spring

Easter comes with cheeks a-glowing
Flowers bloom and streams are flowing,
And the earth
in glad surprise
Opens wide its springtime eyes.

All nature heeds the call of spring
As God awakens everything,
And all that seemed
so dead and still
Experiences a sudden thrill

As springtime lays a magic hand
Across God's vast and fertile land.
Oh, how can anyone
stand by
And watch a sapphire springtime sky,

Or see a fragile flower break through
What just a day ago or two
Seemed barren ground
still hard with frost,
But in God's world no life is lost,

And flowers sleep beneath the ground
But when they hear spring's waking sound
They push themselves
through layers of clay
To reach the sunlight of God's day.

And man, like flowers, too, must sleep
Until he is called from the "darkened deep"
To live in that place
where angels sing
And where there is eternal spring!

The Glory of the Easter Story

In the glorious Easter story
A troubled world can find
Blessed reassurance
And enduring peace of mind.
For though we grow discouraged
In this world we're living in,
There is comfort just in knowing
God has triumphed over sin
For our Saviour's Resurrection
Was God's way of telling men
That in Christ we are eternal
And in Him we live again.
And to know life is unending
And God's love is endless, too,
Makes our daily tasks and burdens
So much easier to do.
For the blessed Easter story
Of Christ the living Lord,
Makes our earthly sorrow nothing
When compared with this reward.

An Easter Meditation

At this holy season
Give us quietness of mind,
Teach us to be patient
And help us to be kind,
Give us reassurance
That You are always near
To guide us and protect us
In this violent world of fear,
Help us all to realize
There is untold strength and power
When we seek the Lord and find Him
In our meditation hour.

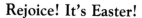

Rejoice! It's Easter!

"Let not your heart be troubled"
Let not your soul be sad
Easter is a time of joy
When all hearts should be glad,
Glad to know that Jesus Christ
Made it possible for men
To have their sins forgiven
And, like Him, to live again.
So at this joyous season
May the wondrous Easter story
Renew our faith so we may be
Partakers of His Glory!

The Miracles of Easter

The sleeping earth awakens,
    The robins start to sing,
The flowers open wide their eyes
    To tell us it is spring,
The bleakness of the winter
    Is melted by the sun,
The tree that looked so stark and dead
-    Becomes a living one.
These miracles of Easter
    Wrought with divine perfection,
Are the blessed reasssurance
    Of our Saviour's Resurrection.

A Special Prayer
for Easter

God, make us aware
   that the Saviour died
And was nailed to a cross
   and crucified
Not to redeem
   just a chosen few
But to save all who ask
   for forgiveness from You.

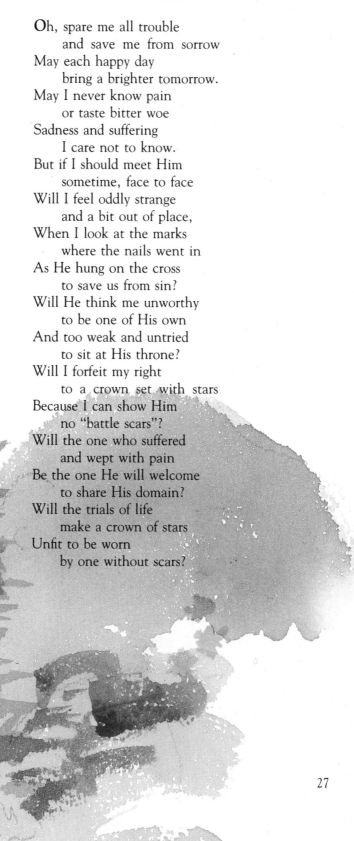

A Crown of Stars

Oh, spare me all trouble
    and save me from sorrow
May each happy day
    bring a brighter tomorrow.
May I never know pain
    or taste bitter woe
Sadness and suffering
    I care not to know.
But if I should meet Him
    sometime, face to face
Will I feel oddly strange
    and a bit out of place,
When I look at the marks
    where the nails went in
As He hung on the cross
    to save us from sin?
Will He think me unworthy
    to be one of His own
And too weak and untried
    to sit at His throne?
Will I forfeit my right
    to a crown set with stars
Because I can show Him
    no "battle scars"?
Will the one who suffered
    and wept with pain
Be the one He will welcome
    to share His domain?
Will the trials of life
    make a crown of stars
Unfit to be worn
    by one without scars?

The Promise of Easter

"Because He lives we too shall live"
We need these seven words above
To help us to endure
The changing world around us
that is dark and insecure,
To help us view the present
as a passing episode,
A troubled, brief encounter
on life's short and troubled road.
For knowing life's eternal
because our Saviour died
And rose again at Easter
after He was crucified
Makes this uncertain present
in a world of sin and strife,
Nothing but a stepping-stone
to a new and better life!

Let Us Pray on This Holy Easter Day

Let our prayer continue
Through a joyous waking spring
In thanking God for everything
A newborn spring can bring.
And in the resurrection
That takes place in nature's sod
Let us understand more fully
The risen Saviour, Son of God.
And let us see the beauty
And the glory and the grace
That surrounds us in the springtime
as the smiling of God's face.
And through a happy springtime
and a summer filled with love
May we walk into the autumn
With our thoughts on God above.
The God who sends the winter
and wraps the earth in death
Will always send the springtime
with an awaking breath
To every flower and leaflet
And to every shrub and tree
And that same God will also send
New life to you and me.

The Easter Story
A Special Narration

He was crucified and buried,
But today the whole world knows
The Resurrection story
Of how Jesus Christ arose.
Some may question it and doubt it,
But they can't explain or say
Why, after countless centuries,
Men still follow Christ today.
And they miss the peace and comfort
That the Easter story brings,
The promise of eternal life
And the hope for better things.
For just to know the Saviour died
To redeem and save all men,
And that because He gave His life,
We, too, shall live again,
Makes all this world's uncertainties,
Its burdens, care, and strife
Seem meaningless when they're compared
To God's eternal life.
And Easter, as it comes each year
To awake the sleeping earth,
Assures mankind that Jesus Christ
Has promised us rebirth.

A Mother's Love Is a Haven in the Storm of Life

A *Mother's Love* is like an island
In life's ocean vast and wide,
A peaceful, quiet shelter
From the restless, rising tide.

A *Mother's Love* is like a fortress
And we seek protection there
When the waves of tribulation
Seem to drown us in despair.

A *Mother's Love*'s a sanctuary
Where our souls can find sweet rest
From the struggle and the tension
Of life's fast and futile quest.

A *Mother's Love* is like a tower
Rising far above the crowd,
And her smile is like the sunshine
Breaking through a threatening cloud.

A *Mother's Love* is like a beacon
Burning bright with faith and prayer,
And through the changing scenes of life
We can find a haven there.

For A *Mother's Love* is fashioned
After God's enduring love,
It is endless and unfailing
Like the love of Him above.

For God knew in His great wisdom
That He couldn't be everywhere,
So He put His little children
In a loving mother's care.

Mother Is a Word Called Love

Mother is a word called love
And all the world is mindful of
The love that's given and shown to others
Is different from the love of Mothers.
For Mothers play the leading roles
In giving birth to little souls,
For though "small souls" are heaven-sent
And we realize they're only lent,
It takes a Mother's loving hands
And her gentle heart that understands
To mold and shape this little life
And shelter it through storm and strife.
No other love than Mother love
Could do the things required of
The one to whom God gives the keeping
Of His wee lambs, awake or sleeping,
So Mothers are a "special race"
God sent to earth to take His place,
And Mother is a lovely name
That even Saints are proud to claim.

Mother's Day Is Remembrance Day

And we pause on the path of the year
To pay honor and worshipful tribute
To the Mother our heart holds dear.
For, whether here or in heaven,
Her love is our haven and guide,
For always the memory of Mother
Is a beacon light shining inside.
Time cannot destroy her memory
And years can never erase
The tenderness and the beauty
Of the love in a Mother's face.
And, when we think of our Mother,
We draw nearer to God above,
For only God in His Greatness
Could fashion a Mother's love.

When I Married You

When I married you, my darling,
I loved you very much,
I thrilled to have you near me
And at the dearness of your touch.
I said no love could ever be
More wonderful than this,
And no thrill could ever equal
The magic of your kiss.
But, darling, I've discovered
That I really never knew
That anyone could love someone
The way I now love you.
For God has blessed our union
With "The Miracle of Love"
And given us a little child
That we are "guardians" of.
And so together, sweetheart,
We've a deeper joy to share,
For God has just entrusted
a small angel to our care.
And this just comes to tell you
I'm as proud as I can be
That the dearest wife and mother
is the girl who married me.

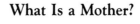

What Is a Mother?

It takes a Mother's Love
to make a house a home,
A place to be remembered,
no matter where we roam.
It takes a Mother's patience
to bring a child up right,
And her courage and her cheerfulness
to make a dark day bright.
It takes a Mother's thoughtfulness
to mend the heart's deep "hurts,"
And her skill and her endurance
to mend little socks and shirts.
It takes a Mother's kindness
to forgive us when we err,
To sympathize in trouble
and bow her head in prayer.
It takes a Mother's wisdom
to recognize our needs
And to give us reassurance
by her loving words and deeds.

Motherhood

The dearest gifts that heaven holds,
    The very finest, too,
Were made into one pattern
    That was perfect, sweet, and true;
The angels smiled, well-pleased, and said:
    "Compared to all the others,
This pattern is so wonderful
    Let's use it just for Mothers!"
And through the years, a Mother
    Has been all that's sweet and good
For there's a bit of God and love,
    In all true Motherhood.

A Mother's Love

A Mother's love is something
    that no one can explain,
It is made of deep devotion
    and of sacrifice and pain.
It is endless and unselfish
    and enduring come what may
For nothing can destroy it
    or take that love away.
It is patient and forgiving
    when all others are forsaking,
And it never fails or falters
    even though the heart is breaking.
It believes beyond believing
    when the world around condemns,
And it glows with all the beauty
    of the rarest, brightest gems.
It is far beyond defining,
    it defies all explanation,
And it still remains a secret
    like the mysteries of creation:
A many-splendored miracle
    man cannot understand
And another wondrous evidence
    of God's tender guiding hand.

A Prayer for Those Lost in Battle

"Give *eternal rest* to them, O Lord"
Whose souls have taken flight
And lead them to a better world
Where there is peace and light.
Grant them *eternal freedom*
From conflict, war, and care,
And fulfill for them Thy prophecy
"There shall be no night there."

A Memorial Day Prayer

They served and fought and died
so that we might be
safe and free,
Grant them, O Lord,
Eternal peace
and give them "The Victory"!
And in these days of unrest,
filled with grave uncertainty,
Let's not forget
The price they paid
to keep our country free . . .
And so, on this Memorial Day,
we offer up a prayer—
May the people of all nations
be united in Thy care,
And grant us understanding
and teach us how to live
So we may lose
our selfish pride
and learn to love and give,
And keep us ever mindful
of the fighting men who sleep
In Arlington and foreign lands
so we may ever keep
The "light of freedom" burning
in their honor through the years
And hear their cry
for peace on earth
resounding in our ears—
Forgive us our transgressions
and "Oh, God, be with us yet"
Lest in our pride
and arrogance
we heedlessly forget.

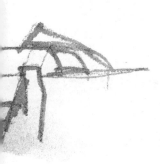

SUMMER

The Best Things

The best things are nearest:
breath in your nostrils,
light in your eyes,
flowers at your feet,
duties at your hand,
the path of Right just before you.
Then do not grasp at the stars,
but do life's plain, common work
as it comes, certain that
daily duties and daily bread
are the sweetest things of life.

The Comfort and Sweetness of Peace

After the clouds, the sunshine,
After the winter, the spring,
After the shower, the rainbow
For life is a changeable thing;
After the night, the morning,
Bidding all darkness cease,
After life's cares and sorrows,
The comfort and sweetness of peace.

The Soul, Like Nature, Has Seasons, Too

When you feel cast down and despondently sad
And you long to be happy and carefree and glad,
Do you ask yourself, as I so often do,
Why must there be days that are cheerless and blue?
Why is the song silenced in the heart that was gay?
And then I ask God, "What makes life this way?"
And His explanation makes everything clear,
The soul has its seasons, the same as the year,
Man, too, must pass through life's autumn of death
And have his heart frozen by winter's cold breath.
But spring always comes with new life and birth
followed by summer to warm the soft earth.
And, oh, what a comfort to know there are reasons
That souls, like nature, must too have their seasons,
Bounteous seasons and barren ones, too,
Times for rejoicing and times to be blue.
For with nothing but "sameness" how dull life would be
For only life's challenge can set the soul free,
And it takes a mixture of both bitter and sweet
To season our lives and make them complete.

The Key to Serenity

When you know
and believe
without question
or doubt
That in all you do
God is there
to help out,
You hold in your hand
the golden key
to peace and joy
and serenity.

Let Daily Prayers
Dissolve Your Cares

We all have cares and problems
    we cannot solve alone
But if we go to God in prayer
    we are never on "our own."
And if we try to stand alone
    we are weak and we will fall,
For God is always greatest
    when we're helpless, lost, and small.
And no day is unmeetable
    if on rising our first thought
Is to thank God for the blessings
    that His loving care has brought.
For there can be no failures
    or hopeless, unsaved sinners
If we enlist the help of God
    who makes all losers winners.
So meet Him in the morning
    and go with Him through the day
And thank Him for His guidance
    each evening when you pray.
And if you follow faithfully
    this daily way to pray
You will never in your lifetime
    face another "hopeless day."
For like a soaring eagle
    you too can rise above
The "storms of life" around you
    on the wings of prayer and love.

The Center of the Flame

In the center of the flame
    there is a hollow place
And nothing can burn
    in this sheltered space.
For the fire builds a wall
    scientific fact claims
And insures a safe area
    in the midst of the flames.
And in the hurricane's fury
    there's a center of peace
Where the winds of destruction
    suddenly cease.
And this same truth prevails
    in life's tribulations
There's an island of calm
    in the soul's meditations:
A place that is quiet
    where we're shielded from harms
Secure in the haven
    of a kind Father's arms
Where the hot flames of anger
    have no power to sear
And the high winds of hatred
    and violence and fear
Lose all the wrath
    and their savage course
Is softly subdued
    as faith weakens force.
So when the fires of life
    burn deep in your heart
And the winds of destruction
    seem to tear you apart
Remember God loves you
    and wants to protect you.
So seek that small haven
    and be guided by prayer
To that place of protection
    within God's loving care.

God's Gifts
Are Bountiful

We ask for a cupful
when the vast sea is ours,
We pick a small rosebud
from a garden of flowers.
Whatever we ask for
falls short of God's giving,
For His greatness exceeds
every facet of living.

I Come to Meet You

I come to Meet You God . . . and as I linger here
    I seem to feel You very near.
A rustling leaf . . . a rolling slope . . .
    speaks to my heart of endless hope.
The sun just rising in the sky,
    the waking birdlings as they fly,
The grass all wet with morning dew
    are telling me I've just met You!
And gently thus the day is born
    and night gives way to breaking morn
And once again I've met You God
    and worshiped on "Your holy sod"
For who can see the dawn break through
    Without a glimpse of heaven and You?
For *who but God could make the day*
    and *softly put the night away.*

A Prayer for the Bride

Oh, God of love look down and bless
This radiant bride with happiness,
And fill her heart with "Love's Sweet Song"
Enough to last her whole life long
And give her patience when things disturb
So she can somehow gently curb
Hasty words in anger spoken,
Leaving two hearts sad and broken.
And give her guidance all through life
And keep her a loving, faithful wife.

Remember These Words

We are gathered together
on this happy day
To stand before God and to reverently say:
I take thee to be my partner for life,
To love and to live with
as husband and wife;
To have and to hold forever, Sweetheart,
Through sickness and health
until death do us part;
To love and to cherish whatever betide,
And in better or worse
to stand by your side . . .
We do this not lightly but solemnly, Lord,
Asking Thy blessing as we live in accord
With Thy holy precepts which
join us in love
And assure us Thy guidance
and grace from above . . .
And grant us, dear Lord, that
"I will" and "I do"
Are words that grow deeper
and more meaningful, too,
Through long, happy years of caring
and sharing,
Secure in the knowledge
that we are preparing
A love that is endless and never
can die
But finds its fulfillment with You
in the "sky."

Love One Another

Love works in ways
that are wondrous and strange,
There is nothing in life
that Love cannot change—
Love is unselfish,
understanding, and kind,
Love sees with the heart
and not with the mind,
And there's no stronger bond
between husband and wife
To insure and secure
a blessed married life
Than to daily seek guidance
from the Father above
And to meet what life brings
with faith, trust and love.

54

The Miracle of Marriage

Marriage is the union of two people in love,
And love is sheer magic for it's woven of
Gossamer dreams enchantingly real
That people in love are privileged to feel.
But the "exquisite ecstasy" that captures the heart
Of two people in love is just a small part
Of the beauty and wonder and miracle of
The growth and fulfillment and evolvement of love.
For only long years of living together
And sharing and caring in all kinds of weather
Both pleasure and pain, the glad and the sad,
Teardrops and laughter, the good and the bad,
Can add new dimensions and lift love above
The rapturous ecstasies of "falling in love."
For ecstasy passes but it is replaced
By something much greater that cannot be defaced,
For what was "in part" has now "become whole"—
For on the "wings of the flesh," love entered the soul!

With Faith in Each Other
and Faith in the Lord

With faith in each other
    and faith in the Lord
May your marriage be blessed
    with love's priceless reward,
For love that endures
    and makes life worth living
Is built on strong faith
    and unselfish giving.
So have faith, and the Lord
    will guide both of you through
The glorious new life
    that is waiting for you.

Another Anniversary!
Another Link of Love!

It only seems like yesterday
That you were a radiant bride
With a proud and happy bridegroom
Standing at your side.
And looking back across the years
On a happy day like this
Brings many treasured memories
As you fondly reminisce.
And while you've had your arguments
And little "tiffs," it's true,
And countless little problems
To vex and worry you,
For every "hurt and heartache"
And perhaps at times some "tears"
You've shared a world of happiness
Throughout your married years.
And looking back on this glad day
You both realize anew
That the sweetest words you ever said
Were just the words, "I do!"

God Bless
Your Anniversary

This happy anniversary proves
    a fact you can't disparage
It takes true love and faith and hope
    to make a happy marriage.
And it takes a lot of praying
    and a devoted man and wife
To keep God ever-present
    in their home and in their life.
And you're a grand example
    and an inspiration, too,
And every married couple
    should be patterned after you.

The Bond of Love Grows Stronger

It takes a special day like this
To just look back and reminisce
And think of all the things you've shared
Since that first day you knew you cared.
Of course things change for that is life
And love between a man and wife
Cannot remain "romantic bliss"
Forever "flavored with a kiss,"
But always there's that bond of love
There's just no explanation of,
And with the "storms" and "trials" it grows
Like flowers do beneath the snows.
Sometimes it's hidden from the sight
Just like the sun gets lost in night,
But always there's that bond of love
There's just no explanation of
And every year that you're together,
Regardless of the "kind of weather"
The bond of love grows that much stronger
Because you've shared it one year longer.

You've Come a Long Way

You've come a long way
    over smooth roads and rough
But you've had each other
    and that was enough,
For even the darkest and
    stormiest weather
Brings a "rainbow of love"
    when you share it together,
And because you have shared
    your smiles and your tears
You've built up "rich treasures"
    in these many years.
For the memories of things
    you've both shared and faced
Are engraved in your hearts
    and they can't be erased,
And life with its problems
    has been but the blending
Of a love that's *divine*
    and therefore *unending*.
For love that endures
    through a long earthly life
And keeps folks together
    as husband and wife
Does not come and go
    with the physical form
And cannot be lost
    in the "sun or the storm,"
For it has become
    an intangible part
Of the soul and the spirit
    as well as the heart,
And because it's eternal
    such love never dies
For it is the kind
    you "take to the skies,"
And the world would be better
    and more lovely by far
If all married couples
    were the kind that you are!

Ideals
Are Like Stars

You can chart
your course in life
with high ideals and love,
For high ideals
are like the stars
that light the sky above.
You cannot ever
reach them,
but lift your heart up high
And your life
will be as shining
as the stars
up in the sky.

62

A Graduate's Prayer

Father, I have knowledge,
so will You show me now
How to use it wisely
and find a way somehow
To make the world I live in
a little better place,
And make life with its problems
a bit easier to face.
Grant me faith and courage
and put purpose in my days,
And show me how to serve Thee
in the most effective ways
So all my education,
my knowledge and my skill,
May find their true fulfillment
as I learn to do Thy Will.
And may I ever be aware
in everything I do
That knowledge comes from learning
and wisdom comes from You.

God Loves Us

We are all
God's children
and He loves us
every one—
He freely
and completely
forgives all
that we have done,
Asking only
if we're ready
to follow where He leads,
Content that
in His wisdom
He will answer
all our needs.

Fathers Are Wonderful People

Fathers are wonderful people
    too little understood,
And we do not sing their praises
    as often as we should.
For, somehow, Father seems to be
    the man who pays the bills,
While Mother binds up little hurts
    and nurses all our ills.
And Father struggles daily
    to live up to "his image"
As protector and provider
    and "hero of the scrimmage."
And perhaps that is the reason
    we sometimes get the notion
That Fathers are not subject
    to the thing we call emotion.
But if you look inside Dad's heart,
    where no one else can see,
You'll find he's sentimental
    and as "soft" as he can be.
But he's so busy every day
    in the gruelling race of life,
He leaves the sentimental stuff
    to his partner and his wife.
But Fathers are just *wonderful*
    in a million different ways,
And they merit loving compliments
    and accolades of praise.
For the only reason Dad aspires
    to fortune and success
Is to make the family proud of him
    and to bring them happiness.
And like our Heavenly Father,
    he's a guardian and a guide,
Someone that we can count on
    to be always on our side.

The Prodigal Son

With riches and youth to squander
The pleasure-bent "prodigal son"
Left the house of his Father
In search of adventure and fun.
And in reckless and riotous living
He wasted his youth and his gold,
And stripped of his earthly possessions
He was hungry and friendless and cold.
And thus he returned to his father
Who met him with arms open wide
And cried, "My son, you are welcome
And a banquet awaits you inside."
Now this story is told to remind us
Not so much of the wandering son
But the *unchanging love* of the father
Who gladly forgave all he'd done.
And the message contained in this story
Is a powerful, wonderful one,
For it shows us our Father in heaven
Waits to welcome each prodigal son.
And whatever have been our transgressions,
God is waiting to welcome us back
And restore us our place in His Kingdom
And give us the joy that we lack.
So wander no longer in darkness,
Let not your return be delayed,
For the door to God is wide open
To welcome "the sheep that have strayed."

Let Your Life Become a Prayer

Sometimes when a light
goes out of our life
and we are left
in darkness
and do not know which way to go,
we must put our hand
into the hand of God
and ask Him to lead us . . .
and if we let our life
become a prayer
until we are strong enough
to stand under the weight
of our own thoughts again,
somehow even the most difficult
hours are bearable.

A Prayer for Independence Day

God bless America and keep us safe and free,
Safe from "all our enemies" wherever they may be.
For enemies are forces that often dwell within,
Things that seem so harmless become a major sin,
Little acts of selfishness grow into lust and greed
And make the love of power our idol and our creed . . .
For all our wealth and progress are as
worthless as can be
Without the faith that made us great
and kept our nation free,
And while it's hard to understand the
complexities of war,
Each one of us must realize that we are fighting for
The principles of freedom and the decency of man,
But all of this must be achieved according
to God's plan.
So help us as Americans to search deep down inside
And discover if the things we do are always justified,
And teach us to walk humbly and closer in Thy ways
And give faith and courage
and put purpose in our days,
And make each one of us aware that each
must do his part
For in the individual is where peace must
have its start.
For a better world to live in where all are
safe and free
Must start with faith and hope
and love deep in the heart of "me."

AUTUMN

A Prayer of Thanks

Thank You, God, for the beauty
    around me everywhere,
The gentle rain and glistening dew,
    the sunshine and the air,
The joyous gift of feeling
    the soul's soft, whispering voice
That speaks to me from deep within
    and makes my heart rejoice.

So Many Reasons to Love the Lord

Thank You, God, for little things
    that come unexpectedly
To brighten up a dreary day
    that dawned so dismally.
Thank You, God, for sending
    a happy thought my way
To blot out my depression
    on a disappointing day.
Thank You, God, for brushing
    the "dark clouds" from my mind
And leaving only "sunshine"
    and joy of heart behind.
Oh, God, the list is endless
    of things to thank You for
But I take them all for granted
    and unconsciously ignore
That everything I think or do,
    each movement that I make,
Each measured, rhythmic heartbeat,
    each breath of life I take
Is something You have given me
    for which there is no way
For me in all my "smallness"
    to in any way repay.

Give Thanks Every Hour

We all have many things to be deeply thankful for,
But God's everlasting promise of life forevermore
Is a reason for thanksgiving every hour of the day
As we walk toward eternal life along "the King's highway."

Things to Be Thankful For

The good, green earth beneath our feet,
The air we breathe, the food we eat,
Some work to do, a goal to win,
A hidden longing deep within
That spurs us on to bigger things
And helps us meet what each day brings,
All these things and many more
Are things we should
be thankful for.
And something else
we should not forget
That people we've known
or heard of or met
By indirection have had
a big part
In molding the thoughts
of the mind and the heart.
And so it's the people
who are like you
That people like me
should give thanks to,
For no one can live
to himself alone
And no one can win
just on his own.
Too bad there aren't
a whole lot more
People like *you*
to be thankful for.

A Heart Full of Thanksgiving

Everyone needs someone
    to be thankful for
And each day of life
    we are aware of this more
For the joy of enjoying
    and the fullness of living
Are found only in hearts
    that are filled with thanksgiving!

Quit Supposin'

Don't start your day by supposin'
    that trouble is just ahead,
It's better to stop supposin'
    and start with a prayer instead,
And make it a prayer of *thanksgiving*
    for the wonderful things God has wrought
Like the beautiful sunrise and sunset,
    "God's gifts" that are free and not bought.
For what is the use of supposin'
    the dire things that could happen to you
And worry about some misfortune
    that seldom if ever comes true?
But instead of just idle supposin'
    step forward to meet each new day
Secure in the knowledge God's near you
    to lead you each step of the way.
For supposin' the worst things will happen
    only helps to make them come true
And you darken the bright, happy moments
    that the dear Lord has given to you.
So if you desire to be happy
    and get rid of the "misery of dread"
Just give up "supposin' the worst things"
    and look for "the best things" instead.

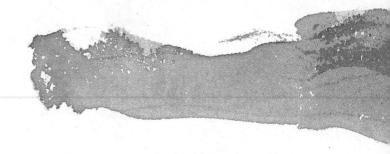

To Know

To know beyond belief that somone cares and hears
Our prayers provides security for the soul, peace
Of mind, and joy of heart that no earthly trials,
Tribulations, sickness, or sorrow can penetrate.
For faith makes it wholly possible to quietly endure
The violent world around us, for in God we are secure!

Yesterday . . . Today . . . and Tomorrow!

Yesterday's dead,
Tomorrow's unborn,
So there's nothing to fear
And nothing to mourn,
For all that is past
And all that has been
Can never return
To be lived once again.
And what lies ahead
Or the things that will be
Are still in God's hands
So it is not up to me
To live in the future
That is God's great unknown,
For the past and the present
God claims for His own.
So all I need do
Is to live for Today
And trust God to show me
The truth and the way.
For it's only the memory
Of things that have been
And expecting tomorrow
To bring trouble again
That fills my today,
Which God wants to bless,
With uncertain fears
And borrowed distress.
For all I need live for
Is this one little minute,
For life's here and now
And eternity's in it.

May the Good Lord Bless
and Keep You Always

To be in God's keeping
    is surely a blessing,
For though life is often
    dark and distressing,
No day is too dark
    and no burden too great
That God in His love
    cannot penetrate,
And to know and believe
    without question or doubt
That no matter what happens
    God is there to help out,
Is to hold in your hand
    "The golden key"
To peace and to joy
    and serenity!

I've Never Seen God

I've never seen God
but I know how I feel,
It's people like you
who make Him "so real."
My God is no stranger,
He's friendly and gay
And He doesn't ask me
to weep when I pray.
It seems that I pass Him
so often each day
In the faces of people
I meet on my way.
He's the stars in the heaven,
a smile on some face,
A leaf on a tree
or a rose in a vase.
He's winter and autumn
and summer and spring
In short, God is every
real, wonderful thing . . .
I wish I might meet Him
much more than I do,
I would if there were
More people like you.

A Golden Day

This has been a golden day
of sweet sadness
That my heart will cherish
long after
The happier hours are forgotten
and time has stilled
our laughter.

The words that make the soul
rejoice
Are spoken by the heart's
"still voice."

The End of the Road
Is But a Bend in the Road

When we feel we have nothing left to give
And we are sure that the "song has ended"
When our day seems over and the shadows fall
And the darkness of night has descended,
Where can we go to find the strength
To valiantly keep on trying,
Where can we find the hand that will dry
The tears that the heart is crying?
There's but one place to go and that is to God
And, dropping all pretense and pride,
We can pour out our problems without restraint
And gain strength with Him at our side.
And together we stand at life's crossroads
And view what we think is the end,
But God has a much bigger vision
And He tells us it's only a bend.
For the road goes on and is smoother,
And the "pause in the song" is a "rest,"
And the part that's unsung and unfinished
Is the sweetest and richest and best.
So rest and relax and grow stronger,
Let go and let God share your load,
Your work is not finished or ended,
You've just come to "a bend in the road."

Give Lavishly! Live Abundantly

The more you give,
    the more you get
The more you laugh,
    the less you fret
The more you do
    unselfishly,
The more you live
    abundantly
The more of everything
    you share,
The more you'll always
    have to spare
The more you love,
    the more you'll find
That life is good
    and friends are kind
For only what
    We give away,
Enriches us
    from day to day.

It's Me Again, God

Remember me, God?
I come every day
Just to talk with You, Lord,
And to learn how to pray.
You make me feel welcome,
You reach out Your hand,
I need never explain
For You understand.
I come to You frightened
And burdened with care
So lonely and lost
And so filled with despair,
And suddenly, Lord,
I'm no longer afraid,
My burden is lighter
And the dark shadows fade.
Oh, God, what a comfort
To know that You care
And to know when I seek You
You will always be there!

A Favorite Prayer

God, open my eyes so I may see
And feel Your presence close to me.
Give me strength for my stumbling feet
As I battle the crowd on life's busy street,
And widen the vision of my unseeing eyes
So in passing faces I'll recognize
Not just a stranger, unloved and unknown,
But a friend with a heart that is much like my own.
Give me perception to make me aware
That scattered profusely on life's thoroughfare
Are the best gifts of God that we daily pass by
As we look at the world with an unseeing eye.

Everybody Everywhere Needs
Somebody Sometime

Everybody, everywhere,
    no matter what his station,
Has moments of deep loneliness
    and quiet desperation,
For this lost and lonely feeling
    is inherent in mankind—
It is just the Spirit speaking
    as God tries again to find
An opening in the "worldly wall"
    man builds against God's touch,
For he feels so self-sufficient
    that he does not need God much,
So he vainly goes on struggling
    to find some explanation
For these disturbing, lonely moods
    of inner isolation.
But the answer keeps eluding him
    for in his selfish, finite mind
He does not even recognize
    that he cannot ever find
The reason for life's emptiness
    unless he learns to share
The problems and the burdens
    that surround him everywhere.
But when his eyes are opened
    and he looks with love at others
He begins to see not strangers
    but understanding brothers.
So open up your hardened hearts
    and let God enter in
He only wants to help you
    a new life to begin
And every day's a good day
    to lose yourself in others
And anytime a good time
    To see mankind as brothers,
And this can only happen
    when you realize it's true
That everyone needs someone
    and that someone is you!

From the Garden of Friendship

There is no garden
    so complete
But roses make
    the place more sweet;
There is no life
    so rich and rare
But one more friend
    can enter there.

87

A Birthday Message for Someone
Who Will Always
Be Young

Some folks grow older with birthdays, it's true,
But others grow nicer as years widen their view,
And a heart that is young lends an aura of grace
That rivals in beauty a young, pretty face.
For no one would notice a few little wrinkles
When a kind, loving heart fills the eyes full of twinkles.
So don't count your years by the birthdays you've had,
But by things you have done to make other folks glad!

A Birthday Meditation

God in His loving and all-wise way
    Makes the heart that once was young and gay
Serene and more gentle and less restless, too,
    Content to remember the joys it once knew.
And all that we sought on the pathway of pleasure
    Becomes but a memory to cherish and treasure.
The fast pace grows slower and the spirit serene,
    And the soul can envision what the eyes
        have not seen.
And so while life's springtime is sweet to recall,
    The autumn of life is the best time of all,
For our wild youthful yearnings all gradually cease
    And God fills our days with beauty and peace!

Stepping-stones

As birthdays come and go
    and years go swiftly by
Each one becomes a "stepping-stone"
    to that "promised land on high."
And I look forward happily
    to that life that never ends
Where we can visit endlessly
    with our loved ones and our friends.

So in these troubled days on earth
    I rejoice to know it's true
That someday I'll spend eternity
    With "angels" just like you.

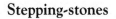

Life's Golden Autumn

Birthdays come and birthdays go
    and with them comes the thought
Of all the happy memories
    that the passing years have brought
And looking back across the years
    it's a joy to reminisce,
For memory opens wide the door
    on a happy day like this,
And with a sweet nostalgia
    we longingly recall
The happy days of long ago
    that seem the best of all.
But time cannot be halted
    in its swift and endless flight
And age is sure to follow youth
    as day comes after night.
And once again it's proven
    that the restless brain of man
Is powerless to alter
    God's great unchanging plan.
But while our step grows slower
    and we grow more tired, too,
The soul goes soaring upward
    to realms untouched and new,
For growing older only means
    the spirit grows serene
And we behold things with our souls
    that our eyes have never seen.
And birthdays are but gateways
    to eternal life above
Where "God's children" live forever
    in the beauty of His love.

A New Sense of God

I find that all that was once possible for me to do
with joyful eagerness and bubbling enthusiasm has somehow
become more difficult. These days I find that the greatest
source of comfort and inner peace and the only thing that can
lift "us" above "our earthly bondage" is the deep sense of
aloneness with God (which is not loneliness), for we only find
true spiritual communion when we are alone and can have direct
communication with God!

Growing Older Is Part of God's Plan

You can't "hold back the dawn"
Or "stop the tides from flowing"
Or "keep a rose from withering"
Or "still a wind that's blowing."
And time cannot be halted
in its swift and endless flight
For age is sure to follow youth
like day comes after night.
For He who sets our span of years
and watches from above
Replaces youth and beauty
with peace and truth and love.
And then our souls are privileged
to see a "hidden treasure"
That in our youth escaped our eyes
in our pursuit of pleasure.
So birthdays are but blessings
that open up the way
To the everlasting beauty
of God's eternal day.

Slowing Down

My days are so crowded and my hours are
So few . . . and I can no longer work fast
like I used to do . . . but I know I must
learn to be satisfied . . . that God has not
completely denied . . . the joy of working at
a much slower pace . . . for as long as He
gives me a little place . . . to work with
Him in His vineyard of love . . . and to know
that He's helping me from above . . . gives
me strength to meet each day . . . as I
travel along life's changing way!

Teach Me

Teach me to give of myself, in whatever way I can,
of whatever I have to give. *Teach me to value
myself, my time, my talents, my purpose, my life,
my meaning in Your world.*

New Beginnings

May your retirement
 turn out to be for you
A time of new beginnings
 and new dimensions, too,
In which you find fulfillment
 of your "creative art"
And joy in every avenue
 of spirit, mind, and heart.

The Autumn of Life

What a wonderful time is life's autumn
    when the leaves of the trees are all gold,
When God fills each day, as He sends it,
    with memories, priceless and old . . .
What a treasure house filled with rare jewels
    are the blessings of year upon year,
When life has been lived as you've lived it
    in a home where God's presence is dear . . .
And may the deep meaning surrounding this day,
    like the "paintbrush" of God up above,
Touch your life with wonderful blessings
    and fill your heart brimful with love!

WINTER

The Mystery and Miracle of His Creative Hand

In the beauty of a snowflake,
Falling softly on the land,
Is the mystery and the miracle
Of God's great, creative hand.

A Christmas Prayer

God, make us aware
that in Thy name
The Holy Christ Child
humbly came
To live on earth
and leave behind
New faith and hope
for all mankind.
And make us aware
that the Christmas story
Is everyone's promise
of eternal glory.

"Glory to God in the Highest"

"Glory to God in the highest
And peace on earth to men"
May the Christmas song
the angels sang
Stir in our hearts again
And bring a new awareness
That the fate of every nation
Is sealed securely in the hand
Of the Maker of Creation.
For man, with all his knowledge,
His inventions and his skill,
Can never go an inch beyond
The holy Father's will.
For all of man's achievements
Are so puny and so small,
Just "ant hills" in the kingdom
Of the God who made us all.
For, greater than the scope of man
And far beyond all seeing,
In Him who made the universe,
Man lives and has his being.

What Would We Face This Christmas Morn
If Jesus Christ Had Not Been Born?

In this world of violence
    and hatred and greed
Where men lust for power
    and scorn those in need,
What could we hope for
    and where could we go
To find comfort and courage
    on this earth below
If in Bethlehem's manger
    Christ had not been born
Many centuries ago
    on that first Christmas morn . . .
For life everlasting
    and eternal glory
Were promised to man
    in the Christmas Story!

"Behold, I Bring You Good Tidings of Great Joy"

"Glad Tidings" herald the Christ Child's birth
"Joy to the World" and "Peace on Earth"
"Glory to God",
let all men rejoice
And hearken once more to the "Angel's Voice."

It matters not who or what you are,
All men can behold "the Christmas star"
For the star that shone is shining still
In the hearts of men
of peace and good will,
It offers the answer to every man's need,
Regardless of color or race or creed.

So, joining together in brotherly love,
Let us worship again our Father above,
And forgetting our own little
selfish desires
May we seek what "the star" of Christmas
inspires.

The Miracle of Christmas

The wonderment
    in a small child's eyes,
The ageless awe
    in the Christmas skies,
The nameless joy
    that fills the air,
The throngs that kneel
    in praise and prayer . . .
These are the things
    that make us know
That men may come
    and men may go,
But none will
    ever find a way
To banish Christ
    from Christmas Day . . .
For with each child
    there's born again
A mystery
    that baffles men.

Each Christmas God Renews
His Promise

Long, long ago in a land far away,
There came the dawn
of the first Christmas Day,
And each year we see that promise reborn
That God gave the world
on that first Christmas morn.
For the silent stars in the timeless skies
And the wonderment
in a small child's eyes,
The Christmas songs the carollers sing,
The tidings of joy
that the Christmas bells ring
Remind us again of that still, silent night
When the heavens shone
with a wondrous light,
And the angels sang of Peace on Earth
And told men of
The Christ Child's birth.
For Christmas is more than a beautiful story,
It's the promise of life
and eternal glory.

Christmas Is a Season for Giving

Christmas is a season
For gifts of every kind,
All the glittering, pretty things
That Christmas shoppers find,
Baubles, beads, and bangles
Of silver and of gold.
Anything and everything
That can be bought or sold
Is given at this season
To place beneath the tree
For Christmas is a special time
For giving lavishly.
But there's one rare and priceless gift
That can't be sold or bought,
It's something poor or rich can give
For it's a loving thought—
And loving thoughts are something
For which no one can pay
And only loving hearts can give
This priceless gift away.

Let Us Keep Christ in Christmas

Christmas is a season
    for joy and merrymaking,
A time for gifts and presents
    for giving and for taking,
A festive, friendly, happy time
    when everyone is gay
And cheer, good will and laughter
    are part of Christmas Day.
For God wants us to be happy
    on the birthday of His Son,
And that is why this season
    is such a joyous one.
For long ago the angels
    rejoiced at Bethlehem
And so down through the ages
    we have followed after them.
But in our celebrations
    of merriment and mirth
Let's not forget the miracle
    of the Holy Christ Child's birth . . .
For in our gay festivities
    It is easy to lose sight
Of the Baby in the manger
    and that Holy silent night . . .
For Christmas in this modern world
    is a very different scene
From the stable and the Christ Child
    so peaceful and serene.
For now we think of Christmas
    as glittering gifts and such,
Things for eager eyes to see
    and reaching hands to touch . . .
But we miss the mighty meaning
    and we lose the greater glory

Of the Holy Little Christ Child
    and the Blessed Christmas Story
If we don't keep Christ in Christmas
    and make His love a part
Of all the joy and happiness
    that fill our home and heart . . .
For without the Holy Christ Child
    what is Christmas but a day
That is filled with empty pleasures
    that will only pass away . . .
But by keeping Christ in Christmas
    we are helping to fulfill
The glad tidings of the angels—
    Peace on earth to men, good will . . .
and the Father up in heaven
    looking down on earth, will say—
You have kept Christ in your Christmas . . .
    now I'll keep you all the way!

The Story of the Christmas Guest

It happened one day at the year's white end . . . two neighbors called on an old-time friend . . . and they found his shop so meager and mean . . . made gay with a thousand boughs of green . . . and Conrad was sitting with face a-shine . . . when he suddenly stopped as he stitched a twine . . . and said, "Old friends, at dawn today . . . when the cock was crowing the night away . . . the Lord appeared in a dream to me . . . and said, 'I am coming your guest to be' . . . so I've been busy with feet astir . . . strewing my shop with branches of fir . . . the table is spread and the kettle is shined . . . and over the rafters the holly is twined . . . and now I will wait for my Lord to appear . . . and listen closely so I will hear . . . His step as He nears my humble place . . . and I open the door and look in His face."

So his friends went home and left Conrad alone . . . for this was the happiest day he had known . . . for, long since, his family had passed away . . . and Conrad had spent a sad Christmas Day . . . but he knew with the Lord as his Christmas guest . . . this Christmas would be the dearest and best . . . and he listened with only joy in his heart . . . and with every sound he would rise with a start . . . and look for the Lord to be standing there . . . in answer to his earnest prayer.

So he ran to the window after hearing a sound . . . but all that he saw on the snow-covered ground . . . was a shabby beggar whose shoes were torn . . . and all of his clothes were ragged and worn . . . So Conrad was touched and went to the door . . . and he said, "Your feet must be frozen and sore . . . and I have some shoes in my shop for you . . . and a coat that will keep you warmer, too" . . . So with grateful heart the man went away . . . but Conrad noticed the time of day . . . he wondered what made the dear Lord so late . . . and how much longer he'd have to wait . . . when he heard a knock and ran to the door . . . but it was only a stranger once more . . . a bent, old crone with a shawl of black . . . a bundle of faggots piled on her back . . . she asked for only a place to rest . . . but her voice seemed to plead, "Don't send me away . . . let me rest for a while on Christmas Day" . . . So Conrad brewed her a steaming cup . . . and told her to sit at the table and sup.

But after she left he was filled with dismay . . . for he saw that the hours were passing away . . . and the Lord had not come as He said He would . . . and Conrad felt sure he had misunderstood . . . when out of the stillness he heard a cry . . . "Please help me and tell me where am I" . . . So again he opened his friendly door . . . and stood disappointed as twice before . . . it was only a child who had wandered away . . . and was lost from her family on Christmas Day . . . Again Conrad's heart was heavy and sad . . . but he knew he should make this little child glad . . . so he called her in and wiped her tears . . . and quieted all her childish fears . . . then he led her back to her home once more . . . but as he entered his own darkened door . . . he knew that the Lord was not coming today . . . for the hours of Christmas had passed away.

So he went to his room and knelt down to pray . . . and he said, "Dear Lord, why did You delay . . . what kept You from coming to call on me . . . For I wanted so much Your face to see" . . . when soft in the silence a voice he heard . . . "Lift up your head for I kept My word . . . Three times My shadow crossed your floor . . . three times I came to your lonely door . . . for I was the Beggar with bruised cold feet . . . I was the Woman you gave to eat . . . and I was the Child on the homeless street."

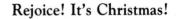

Rejoice! It's Christmas!

May the holy remembrance
    of the first Christmas Day
Be our reassurance
    Christ is not far away.
For on Christmas He came
    to walk here on earth,
So let us find joy
    in the news of His birth.

And let us find comfort
    and strength for each day
In knowing that Christ
    walked this same earthly way.
So He knows all our needs
    and He hears every prayer
And He keeps all "His children"
    always safe in His care.
And whenever we're troubled
    and lost in despair
We have but to seek Him
    and ask Him in prayer
To guide and direct us
    and help us to bear
Our sickness and sorrow,
    our worry and care.
So once more at Christmas
    let the whole world rejoice
In the knowledge He answers
    every prayer that we voice.

A Prayer for Christmas

God give us eyes this Christmas
    to see the Christmas Star,
And give us ears to hear the song
    of angels from afar.
And, with our eyes and ears attuned
    for a message from above,
Let "Christmas Angels" speak to us
    of hope and faith and love.
Hope to light our pathway
    when the way ahead is dark,
Hope to sing through stormy days
    with the sweetness of the lark,
Faith to trust in things unseen
    and know beyond all seeing
That it is in our Father's love
    we live and have our being,
And *love* to break down barriers
    of color, race, and creed,
Love to see and understand
    and help all those in need.

Yesterday and Tomorrow

There are two days about
which nobody should ever worry,
and these are yesterday
and tomorrow.

So, with only today to cope with,
the burden becomes lighter
for nobody ever stumbled
under the burden of today.
It is only when
they add yesterdays and tomorrows
to the load they are carrying,
that it becomes unbearable.

The Great Tomorrow

There is always a Tomorrow. Tomorrow belongs as much to you as it does to me. The dawn of a new day means the dawn of a new life; we cannot peer into its storehouse but the very impenetrable mystery which enwraps the ever approaching Tomorrow, is the one thing that keeps the fires of hope constantly burning.

No matter what our yesterdays have been tomorrow may be different. As long as we have life the fires of hope cannot die out; the flame may burn low but at the thought of a new day the flame which seemed dead, leaps forward and the sparks once more fly upward to spur us on.

Even if our today is filled with sadness and defeat—who can foretell what the next day will bring to us? Let us all eagerly await what destiny will deal us. We speak of man meeting his fate and we speak truthfully for every day we see life converged to life.

Tomorrow may hold your fate—Tomorrow may mean your victory. The great joy of expectation—the wonderment of an unknown realm— the splendor of the vast unlimitable future—all lie in the eternal Tomorrow—the day which makes life worth living.

A New Year! A New Day! A New Life!

Not only on New Year's
but all the year through
God gives us a chance to begin life anew,
For each day at dawning we have but to pray
That all the mistakes that we made yesterday
Will be blotted out and forgiven by grace,
For God in His love will completely efface
All that is past and He'll grant a new start
To all who are truly repentant at heart.
And well may man pause in awesome-like wonder
That our Father in heaven
who dwells far asunder
Could still remain willing to freely forgive
The shabby, small lives we so selfishly live
And still would be mindful of sin-ridden man
Who constantly goes on defying God's plan—
But this is the gift
of God's limitless love,
A gift that we all are so unworthy of,
But God gave it to us and all we need do
Is to ask God's forgiveness and begin life anew.

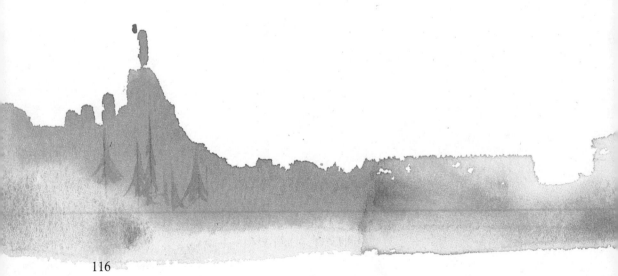

A New Beginning

It doesn't take a new year
to begin our lives anew—
God grants us new beginnings
each day the whole year through,
So never be discouraged
for there comes daily to all men
The chance to make another start
and begin all over again!

A Pattern for the New Year

"Love one another as I have loved you"
May seem impossible to do
But if you will try to trust and believe,
Great are the joys that you will receive.
For love makes us patient, understanding, and kind,
And we judge with our heart and not with our mind.
For as soon as love enters the heart's opened door,
The faults we once saw are not there anymore,
And the things that seemed wrong begin to look right
When viewed in the softness of love's gentle light.
For love works in ways that are wondrous and strange
And there is nothing in life that love cannot change,
And all that God promised will someday come true
When you love one another the way He loved you.

Show Me the Way

God, help me in my own small way
To somehow do something each day
To show You that I love You best
And that my faith will stand each test.
And let me serve You every day
And feel You near me when I pray
Oh, hear my prayer, dear God above,
And make me worthy of Your love!

The Legend of the Valentine

The story of Saint Valentine
Is a legend, it is true,
But legends are delightful
And very lovely, too.

And the legend of Saint Valentine
Imprisoned in a cell
Thinking of his little flock
He had always loved so well
And, wanting to assure them
Of his friendship and his love,
He picked a bunch of violets
And sent them by a dove.

And on the violets' velvet leaves
He pierced these lines divine
That simply said "I love you"
And "I'm your Valentine."
So through the years that followed
From that day unto this
Folks still send messages of love
And seal them with a kiss.

Because a saint in prison
Reached outside his bars one day
And picked a bunch of violets
And sent them out to say
That faith and love can triumph,
No matter where you are,
For faith and love are greater
Than the strongest prison bar.

I Think of You and
I Pray for You, Too

Often during a busy day
I pause for a minute
to silently pray,
I mention the names
of those I love
And treasured friends
I am fondest of.
For it doesn't matter
where we pray
If we honestly mean
the words that we say,
For God is always
listening to hear
The prayers that are made
by a heart that's sincere.

So We Might Know!

Perhaps "this" was a vision
of what human love can be

When it's fashioned out of
sweetness and tender sympathy.

For such love has all the qualities
of an eternal light

That keeps the garments of the soul
Clean and pure and bright.

And so think this "shadow"
was not the "herald of night"

But an Ambassador of love
"that maketh all things right!"

Deep in My Heart

Happy little memories
Go flitting through my mind
And in all my thoughts and memories
I always seem to find
The picture of your face, dear,
The memory of your touch
And all the other little things
I've come to love so much,
You cannot go beyond my thoughts
Or leave my love behind
Because I keep you in my heart
And forever on my mind
And though I may not tell you
I think you know it's true
That I find daily happiness
In the very thought of you.

124

Happiness

Across the years we've met in dreams
And shared each other's hopes and schemes,
We knew a friendship rich and rare
And beautiful beyond compare.
But you reached out your arms for more
To catch what you were yearning for
But little did you think or guess
That one can't capture happiness,
Because it's unrestrained and free
Unfettered by reality.

If I Had Loved You Then

If I had known you way back when
I might have loved you even then
But oh, what a difference there
would have been—If instead of
now, I had loved you then—

Our love might have burned
with a brighter flame
We'd have toasted our fame
in bubbling champagne

We'd have loved and got lost
in a gay world of fun
And now our young love
Would be over and done—

But meeting each other
in the "gold autumn haze"
Has brought deeper meaning
to the last golden days.

A Night Song

In the night I send a song,
    That song dear, is of you;
Every soul is crying out,
    A message dear, for you.

The stars up in the heaven,
    They seem to understand,
They know that I am calling
    Into a far-off land.

The clouds glide by in glory,
    They smile at me and say
That you are thinking of me, too,
    In just the same sweet way.

Merrily the moon winks on,
    It winked at you, I know,
For the greeting that it gave me,
    Was just enough to show.

Old night-time brings me nearer
    to one I love so well
And twinkling stars and moonbeams,
    Ne'er get a chance to tell.

And although we are far apart,
    Your face I almost see,
For stars that take your message
    Are smiling back at me.

The night you love is my night too,
    You're king and I am queen,
For night is God's and free to all,
    Where man is king of dreams.

Where There Is Love

Where there is love
    the heart is light,
Where there is love
    the day is bright,
Where there is love
    there is a song
To help when things
    are going wrong . . .

Where there is love
    there is a smile
To make all things
    seem more worthwhile . . .
Oh, blest are they
    who walk in love . . .
They also walk with God above.